[QUOTABLE WISDOM]

•

The Saints

QUOTABLE WISDOM

WISDOM

•

The Saints

Edited by
CAROL KELLY-GANGI

FALL RIVER PRESS

New York

FALL RIVER PRESS

New York

An Imprint of Sterling Publishing
387 Park Avenue South
New York, NY 10016

Compilation © 2014 by Fall River Press
Originally published in 2009 as *The Essential Wisdom of the Saints.*

ISBN 978-1-4549-1119-7

Distributed in Canada by Sterling Publishing
$^c/_o$ Canadian Manda Group, 165 Dufferin Street
Toronto, Ontario, Canada M6K 3H6
Distributed in the United Kingdom by GMC Distribution Services
Castle Place, 166 High Street, Lewes, East Sussex, England BN7 1XU
Distributed in Australia by Capricorn Link (Australia) Pty. Ltd.
P.O. Box 704, Windsor, NSW 2756, Australia

For information about custom editions, special sales, and premium
and corporate purchases, please contact Sterling Special Sales at
800-805-5489 or specialsales@sterlingpublishing.com.

Manufactured in the United States of America

2 4 6 8 10 9 7 5 3 1

www.sterlingpublishing.com

Contents

*To Mom and Dad with love and
special gratitude for passing on
your lifelong devotion to the Saints*

Introduction

> It is difficult to become a saint. Difficult, but not
> impossible. The road to perfection is long, as long
> as one's lifetime. Along the way, consolation becomes
> rest; but as soon as your strength is restored, you
> must diligently get up and resume the trip.
>
> —*St. Padre Pio*

The path to sainthood is undoubtedly a long one. The process begins with an investigation initiated by a local bishop into the candidate's life and writings in search of evidence of what the Church calls heroic virtue. At this point, the candidate may publicly be called a "Servant of God." If the reviewing panel of theologians and cardinals approves of the case presented by the bishop, the pope may deem the candidate as "Venerable," meaning the person has led a life of sanctity and is a role model of Catholic virtue. Beatification is the next step in the process. After further investigation and indisputable evidence of post-humous miracles that occurred through the intercession of the candidate, the Venerable may be beatified and then called Blessed, at which point limited public veneration may be paid to him or her. (A caveat exists in cases of martyrdom, however. A martyr, someone who voluntarily dies for his or her faith, may be beatified without proof of a posthumous miracle.) After even more investigation and proof of additional miracles, a Blessed may be canonized and declared an official Saint, at which point he or she may be venerated universally in the Church.

Despite the fact that this arduous process can take decades or even centuries to complete, many have successfully traveled the road to sainthood. In fact, the Catholic Church has canonized more than 3,000 saints, though the figure soars to about 10,000 if one includes the saints that have been recognized by the Church in one way or another over the centuries prior to saints being officially canonized. Today, the canonization process is alive and well. Pope John Paul II canonized an astounding 482 saints during his papacy, and now he has begun the journey himself, with his own beatification process underway.

The Saints: Quotable Widsom gathers together more than three hundred quotations from the earliest saints to those canonized within the last decade. The selections are as varied as the saints themselves—and range in literary quality from childlike simplicity to sophisticated eloquence. Whatever their background or station in life, each saint conveys a fervent love for God and humankind, and an unconditional desire to serve Him. In these selections, St. Teresa of Avila extols the virtue of humility; St. Vincent de Paul reminds us to be merciful; St. Francis of Assisi prays for the strength to endure suffering; while St. Patrick marvels at his own conversion. The saints also exchange views on such topics as how to pray; the need for charity; the importance of forgiveness; the pitfalls of the material world; and even offer insights into sainthood itself.

So get ready to journey along with the saints. Through their words they prove now, as through the ages, ready to inspire, guide, and challenge us as they illuminate their joys and disappointments; their spiritual bliss and perseverance; their sanctity and humanity.

—*Carol Kelly-Gangi*

God the Father, the Son, and the Holy Spirit

My soul, have you found what you are looking for? You were looking for God, and you have discovered that He is the supreme being, and that you could not possibly imagine anything more perfect. You have discovered that this supreme being is life itself, light, wisdom, goodness, eternal blessedness and blessed eternity.

—*St. Anselm of Canterbury*

I know God. He is a father, a mother, who in order to be happy must have his child upon His knee, resting on His heart.

—*St. Thérèse of Lisieux*

When the heart is pure it cannot help loving, because it has discovered the source of love which is God.

—*St. John Vianney*

This is what you should think, if you wish to see God: "God is Love," What face has love? What form has it? What height? What feet? What hands? No one can say. Yet it has feet, for they lead to the Church; it has hands, for they care for the poor; it has eyes, for through them the needy one is known.

—*St. Augustine*

Let us love God, but with the strength of our arms, in the sweat of our brow.

—*St. Vincent de Paul*

Our thoughts ought instinctively to fly upwards from animals, men, and natural objects to their Creator. If things created are so full of loveliness, how resplendent with beauty must be He who made them! The wisdom of the Worker is apparent in His handiwork.

—*St. Anthony of Padua*

Imagine a man in whom the tumult of the flesh goes silent, in whom the images of earth, of water, of air, and of the skies cease to resound. His soul turns quiet and, self-reflecting no longer, it transcends itself. Dreams and visions end. So too does all speech and every gesture, everything in fact which comes to be only to pass away. All these things cry out: "We did not make ourselves. It is the Eternal One who made us."

—St. Augustine

I was like a stone lying in the deep mire; and He that is mighty came, and in His mercy lifted me up, and verily raised me aloft and placed me on the top of the wall.

—St. Patrick of Ireland

It is true that the voice of God, having once fully penetrated the heart, becomes strong as the tempest and loud as the thunder; but before reaching the heart it is as weak as a light breath which scarcely agitates the air. It shrinks from noise, and is silent amid agitation.

—St. Ignatius of Loyola

He who desires nothing but God is rich and happy.

—St. Alphonsus Liguori

If, then, you are looking for the way by which you should go, take Christ, because He Himself is the way.

—St. Thomas Aquinas

When we speak about wisdom, we are speaking of Christ.
When we speak about virtue, we are speaking of Christ.
When we speak about justice, we are speaking of Christ.
When we speak about peace, we are speaking of Christ.
When we speak about truth and life and redemption,
  we are speaking of Christ.

—St. Ambrose of Milan

Whoever does not seek the cross of Christ doesn't seek the glory of Christ.

—St. John of the Cross

We adore you, Christ, here and in all your churches which are in the whole world, and we bless you because by your holy cross you have redeemed the world.

—*St. Francis of Assisi*

Be not afraid to tell Jesus that you love Him; even though it be without feeling, this is the way to oblige Him to help you, and carry you like a little child too feeble to walk.

—*St. Thérèse of Lisieux*

If I am distracted, Holy Communion helps me become recollected. If opportunities are offered by each day to offend my God, I arm myself anew each day for the combat by reception of the Eucharist. If I am in need of special light and prudence in order to discharge my burdensome duties, I draw nigh to my Savior and seek counsel and light from Him.

—*St. Thomas More*

Those who guide souls should realize that the principal agent and guide and motive force in this matter is not them but the Holy Spirit, who never fails in His care for people; they are only instruments to guide people to perfection by faith and the law of God, according to the spirit that God is giving to the individual person.

—*St. John of the Cross*

The word Paraclete signifies comforter or advocate; now both these offices imply especially the exercise of goodness, and goodness is a peculiar attribute of God the Holy Ghost, so He is said to be our Comforter in trouble and our Advocate in blessings.

—*St. Thomas Aquinas*

The Spirit works, the Son fulfills His ministry, and the Father approves; and man is thus brought to full salvation.

—*St. Irenaeus*

Love

Too late have I loved you, O Beauty so ancient and so new, too late have I loved you! You were with me, but I was not with you. You cried out and pierced my deafness. You enlightened my blindness. I tasted you and I am hungry for you. You touched me, and I am afire with longing for your embrace.

—St. Augustine

The more we love God, the more we will want to love Him.

—St. Joaquina

We must fear God out of love, not love Him out of fear.

—St. Francis de Sales

If I give all I possess to the poor and surrender my body to the flames, but have not love, I gain nothing.

—*St. Paul*

To love God you need three hearts in one—a heart of fire for Him, a heart of flesh for your neighbor, and a heart of bronze for yourself.

—*St. Benedict Joseph Labre*

At last I have found my calling! My calling is love!

—*St. Thérèse of Lisieux*

The interior life is like a sea of love in which the soul is plunged and is, as it were, drowned in love. Just as a mother holds her child's face in her hands to cover it with kisses, so does God hold the devout man.

—*St. John Vianney*

You should have an equal love for and an equal forgetfulness of all persons, whether relatives or not, and withdraw your heart from relatives as much as from others, and in some ways even more for fear that flesh and blood might be quickened by the natural love that is ever alive among kin, and must always be mortified for the sake of spiritual perfection.

—St. John of the Cross

To love God as He ought to be loved, we must be detached from all temporal love. We must love nothing but Him, or if we love anything else, we must love it only for His sake.

—St. Peter Claver

I shall always be grateful to our Lord for turning earthly friendships into bitterness for me, because, with a nature like mine, I could so easily have fallen into a snare and had my wings clipped; and then how should I have been able to "fly away and find rest"? I don't see how it's possible for a heart given over to such earthly affections to attain any intimate union with God.

—St. Thérèse of Lisieux

Love for our neighbor consists of three things: to desire the greater good of everyone; to do what good we can when we can; to bear, excuse, and hide other's faults.

—*St. John Vianney*

Love is the fusion of two souls in one in order to bring about mutual perfection.

—*St. Teresa of the Andes*

Let us force ourselves to be affectionate, gentle, and humble in our intercourse with all, especially with those whom God has given us as our companions, such, for instance, as those of our household. And never let us consent to be of the number of those who, out of their own house, appear like Angels, but are more like devils at home.

—*St. Francis de Sales*

We are born to love, we live to love, and we will die to love still more.

—*St. Joseph Cafasso*

LOVE

Souls well-beloved of my soul, my eyes ardently desire to behold you; my arms expand to embrace you; my lips sigh for your kisses; all the life that remains to me is consumed with waiting for you. How can I forget those whom I have placed like a seal upon my heart?

—St. Anselm of Canterbury, to his family

It is well known that I had neither riches, nor talent, nor external charm, but I have always loved, and I have loved with all the strength of my heart.

—St. Mary Euphrasia Pelletier

We cannot separate love for God from love for man. We acknowledge God easily, but our brother? Those with whom we do not identify in his background, education, race, complexion. We could not have imagined that love for God could be so hard.

—St. Edith Stein

Without love, deeds, even the most brilliant, count as nothing.

—St. Thérèse of Lisieux

The more we know of men, the less we love them. It is the contrary with God; the more we know of Him, the more we love Him.

—St. John Vianney

There is only one thing to do here below: to love Jesus, to win souls for Him so that He may be loved. Let us seize with jealous care every last opportunity of self-sacrifice. Let us refuse Him nothing—He does so want our love!

—St. Thérèse of Lisieux

Without hesitancy, therefore, let us love our enemies, let us do good to those who hate us, and let us pray for those who persecute us.

—St. Augustine

Let us love the one who offends us since this great God has not ceased to love us even though we have offended Him very much. Thus the Lord is right in wanting all to pardon the wrongs done to them.

—*St. Teresa of Avila*

Therefore once for all this short command is given to you. "Love and do what you will." If you keep silent, keep silent by love; if you speak, speak by love; if you correct, correct by love; if you pardon, pardon by love: let love be rooted in you, and from the root nothing but good can grow.

—*St. Augustine*

The good God does not need years to accomplish His work of love in a soul; one ray from His Heart can, in an instant, make His flower bloom for eternity.

—*St. Thérèse of Lisieux*

No pilgrim soul can worthily love God. But when a soul does everything possible and trusts in divine mercy, why would Jesus reject such a spirit? Has He not commanded us to love God according to our strength? If you have given and consecrated everything to God, why be afraid?

—*St. Padre Pio*

Serving God

I realized that our Lord does not call those who are worthy, but those whom He will.

—*St. Thérèse of Lisieux*

❦

I will often consider myself as an instrument which is of no use except in the hands of the workman. Hence I must await the orders of Providence before acting and be careful to accomplish them when known.

—*St. Jean-Baptiste de La Salle*

❦

Lord, you are the one who acts. I am not even an instrument in your hands, as others say. You alone are the one who does all, and I am nothing more than a spectator of the great and wonderful works that you know how to accomplish.

—*St. Frances Xavier Cabrini*

❦

Man is created to praise, reverence, and serve God our Lord, and by this means to save his soul. All other things on the face of the earth are created for man to help him fulfill the end for which he is created. . . . Therefore we must make ourselves indifferent to all created things, in so far as it is left to the choice of our free will and is not forbidden. Acting accordingly, for our part, we should not prefer health to sickness, riches to poverty, honor to dishonor, a long life to a short one. And so in all things we should desire and choose only those things that will best help us attain the end for which we are created.

—St. Ignatius of Loyola

God is served only when He is served according to His will.

—St. Padre Pio

Do not undertake any course of action, not even the most lowly and insignificant, without first offering it to God.

—St. Padre Pio

Try interrupting the meditations of someone who is very attached to her spiritual exercises and you will see her upset, flustered, taken aback. A person who has this true freedom will leave her prayer, unruffled, gracious toward the person who has unexpectedly disturbed her, for to her it's all the same—serving God by meditating or serving Him by responding to her neighbor. Both are the will of God, but helping the neighbor is necessary at that particular moment.

—St. Francis de Sales

The Lord measures our perfection neither by the multitude nor the magnitude of our deeds, but by the manner in which we perform them.

—St. John of the Cross

As the years pass, and as eternity approaches, we must double our courage, and raise our spirit to God, serving Him with the utmost diligence in all the duties of our Christian vocation or profession.

—St. Padre Pio

Though the path is plain and smooth for men of good will, he who walks it will not travel far, and will do so only with difficulty, if he does not have good feet: that is, courage and a persevering spirit.

—St. John of the Cross

This union of my soul with God is my wealth in poverty and joy in deepest afflictions.

—St. Elizabeth Ann Seton

For what else are the servants of God than His singers, whose duty it is to lift up the hearts of men and move them to spiritual joy?

—St. Francis of Assisi

Yes, it's true; they jump on me like hyenas, they squeeze my hand in a vice-like grip, they pull my arms, they crowd around me in order to touch me; I become bewildered, and have to be severe. I don't like it either, but if I didn't behave that way, they would kill me!

—St. Padre Pio

Society, wounded with the sores of evil, is Lazarus. We are the dogs who must draw near to cure with our tongues—our preaching—by which we lick with the milk and honey of kindness and gentleness, healing not aggravating the evils that afflict humankind.

—St. Anthony of Padua

Reprimand and rebuke should be accepted as healing remedies for vice and as conducive to good health. From this it is clear that those who pretend to be tolerant because they wish to flatter—those who thus fail to correct sinners—actually cause them to suffer supreme loss and plot the destruction of that life which is their true life.

—St. Basil the Great

O my God, I give you my word that I shall preach, write and circulate good books and pamphlets in abundance, so as to drown evil in a flood of good.

—*St. Anthony Mary Claret*

Preach always. If necessary use words.

—*St. Francis of Assisi*

If I had been a man I would have been a great preacher.

—*St. Teresa of Avila*

My object in pronouncing my vows is to embrace Poverty, under whose roof I desire to live and die; Chastity, so lovable and so beautiful, that I truly find all my happiness in cultivating it, and above all, Obedience, the sure refuge and safeguard of my soul.

—*St. Elizabeth Ann Seton*

No one ought to consider himself a true servant of God who is not tried by many temptations and trials. Temptations overcome are a sort of betrothal ring God gives the soul.

—*St. Francis of Assisi*

Every Christian who is a true imitator and follower of the Nazarene can and must call himself a second Christ and show forth most clearly in his life the entire image of Christ. Oh, if only all Christians were to live up to their vocation, this very land of exile would be changed into a paradise.

—*St. Padre Pio*

God does not require of us the martyrdom of the body; He requires only the martyrdom of the heart and the will.

—*St. John Vianney*

I will take no unnecessary walks.

I will make exactingly careful use of my time.

When the salvation of souls is at stake I will always be ready to act, to suffer, and to humble myself.

May the charity and gentleness of St. Francis de Sales inform my every action.

I will always be content with the food set before me unless it is really harmful to my health.

I will always add water to my wine and drink it only for reasons of health.

Since work is a powerful weapon against the enemies of my salvation I will take only five hours sleep a night. During the day, especially after dinner, I will take no rest, except in case of illness.

Every day I will devote some time to meditation and spiritual reading.

During the day I will make a short visit, or at least a prayer, to the Blessed Sacrament. My preparation for Mass shall last at least a quarter of an hour and so shall my thanksgiving.

Outside the confessional and save in cases of strict necessity I will never stop to talk to women.

—*St. John Bosco*

Cast yourself into the arms of God and be very sure that if He wants anything of you, He will fit you for the work and give you strength.

—*St. Philip Neri*

Try to serve the Lord with all your heart and with all your will. He will always bless you more than you deserve.

—*St. Padre Pio*

Just as every sort of gem when cast in honey becomes brighter and more sparkling, so each person becomes more acceptable and fitting in his own vocation when he sets that vocation in the context of devotion. Through devotion family cares become more peaceful, mutual love between husband and wife becomes more sincere, the service we owe the prince becomes more faithful, and our work, no matter what it is, becomes more pleasant and agreeable.

—*St. Francis de Sales*

I have promised God that until my last breath I shall have lived for my poor young people. I study for you, I work for you, I am also ready to give my life for you. Take note that whatever I am, I have been so entirely for you, day and night, morning and evening, at every moment.

—St. John Bosco

Every moment comes to us pregnant with a command from God, only to pass on and plunge into eternity, there to remain forever what we have made it.

—St. Francis de Sales

Prayer, Faith, and Hope

Everything that one turns in the direction of God is a prayer.

—St. Ignatius of Loyola

For me, prayer means launching out of the heart towards God; it means lifting up one's eyes, quite simply, to Heaven, a cry of grateful love from the crest of joy or the trough of despair; it's a vast, supernatural force which opens out my heart, and binds me close to Jesus.

—St. Thérèse of Lisieux

Have patience in persevering in the holy exercise of meditation, and be content to progress in slow steps until you have legs to run and wings with which to fly.

—St. Padre Pio

Acquire the habit of speaking to God as if you were alone with God. Speak with familiarity and confidence as to your dearest and most loving friend. Speak of your life, your plans, your troubles, your joys, your fears. In return, God will speak to you—not that you will hear audible words in your ears, but words that you will clearly understand in your heart.

—St. Alphonsus Liguori

The body is our cell, and the soul is a hermit who stays within in the cell for praying to the Lord and for meditating on Him.

—St. Francis of Assisi

Prayer is the best weapon we have; it is a key that opens God's heart. You must speak to Jesus, not only with your lips, but also with your heart; actually, on certain occasions, you should speak with only your heart.

—St. Padre Pio

Aspire to God with short but frequent outpourings of the heart; admire His bounty; invoke His aid; cast yourself in spirit at the foot of His cross; adore His goodness; treat with Him of your salvation; give Him your whole soul a thousand times in the day.

—St. Francis de Sales

Give some time, if it is only half an hour in every day, to devotional reading, which is as necessary to the well ordering of the mind as the hand of the gardener is to prevent weeds destroying your favorite flowers.

—St. Elizabeth Ann Seton

Countless numbers are deceived in multiplying prayers. I would rather say five words devoutly with my heart than five thousand which my soul does not relish with affection and understanding.

—St. Edmund the Martyr

The best preparation for prayer is to read the lives of the saints, not from mere curiosity, but quietly and with recollection a little at a time. And to pause whenever you feel your heart touched with devotion.

—*St. Philip Neri*

In the spiritual life, the faster we run, the less tired we feel; actually, peace, the prelude to eternal happiness, will come to us, will render us happy and strong, provided that, living in this fashion, we mortify ourselves, and allow Jesus to live in us.

—*St. Padre Pio*

I say very simply to God what I wish to say, without composing beautiful sentences, and he always understands me.

—*St. Thérèse of Lisieux*

All I need is a quiet corner where I can talk to God each day as if there were nothing else to do. I try to make myself a tool for God. Not for myself, but only for Him.

—*St. Edith Stein*

Silence is a gift of God, to let us speak more intimately with God.

—*St. Vincent Pallotti*

No matter how much our interior progress is ordered, nothing will come of it unless by divine aid. Divine aid is available to those who seek it from their hearts, humbly and devoutly; and this means to sigh for it, in this valley of tears, through fervent prayer.

—*St. Bonaventure*

Contemplation is nothing else but a secret, peaceful and loving infusion of God, which, if admitted, will set the soul on fire with the Spirit of love.

—*St. John of the Cross*

If you were to judge by the poems I write you might think that I have been inundated with spiritual consolation, that I am a child for whom the veil of faith is almost rent asunder. But it is not a veil. It is a wall that reaches to the very heavens, shutting out the starry skies. I feel no joy, I sing only of what I wish to believe.

—*St. Thérèse of Lisieux*

The walls of our monasteries enclose a narrow space. To erect the structure of holiness in it, one must dig deep and build high, must descend into the depths of the dark night of one's own nothingness in order to be raised up high into the sunlight of divine love and compassion.

—*St. Edith Stein*

Prayer reveals to souls the vanity of earthly goods and pleasures. It fills them with light, strength and consolation, and gives them a foretaste of the calm bliss of our heavenly home.

—*St. Rose of Viterbo*

If the prayer of a single person is so powerful, much more so is the prayer that is offered with many other people. The sinewy strength of such a prayer and the confidence that God will hear it is far greater than you can have for the prayer you offer privately at home.

—St. John Chrysostom

Man has to believe others in matters that he cannot know perfectly by himself. Now no one is to be believed as much as God is. Thus, those who will not believe the statements of faith are not wise, but foolish and proud.

—St. Thomas Aquinas

We should submit our reason to the truths of faith with the humility and simplicity of a child.

—St. Alphonsus Liguori

I know that you can cling by sheer faith, without seeing or thinking anything.

—St. Teresa of Avila

Faith lifts the staggering soul on one side, Hope supports it on the other. Experience says it must be, and Love says let it be.

—*St. Elizabeth Ann Seton*

What made the holy apostles and martyrs endure fierce agony and bitter torments, except faith, and especially faith in the resurrection?

—*St. Fidelis of Sigmaringen*

Understanding is the reward given by faith. Do not try to understand in order to believe, but believe in order to understand.

—*St. Augustine*

We can't have full knowledge all at once. We must start by believing; then afterwards we may be led on to master the evidence for ourselves.

—*St. Thomas Aquinas*

Do not ever lose heart when the tempest rages; place all your trust in the Heart of the most gentle Jesus. Pray and I might add, devoutly pester the divine Heart.

—St. Padre Pio

I will go peaceably and firmly to the Catholic Church: for if Faith is so important to our salvation, I will seek it where true Faith first began, seek it among those who received it from God Himself.

—St. Elizabeth Ann Seton

O man, believe in God with all your might, for hope rests on faith, love on hope, and victory on love; the reward will follow victory, the crown of life the reward, but the crown is the essence of things eternal.

—St. Nicholas of Flue

Hope always draws the soul from the beauty that is seen to what is beyond, always kindles the desire for the hidden through what is perceived.

—St. Gregory of Nyssa

Live in faith and hope, though it be in darkness, for in this darkness God protects the soul. Cast your care upon God for you are His and He will not forget you. Do not think that He is leaving you alone, for that would be to wrong Him.

—St. John of the Cross

Hope, O my soul, hope. You know neither the day nor the hour. Watch carefully, for everything passes quickly, even though your impatience makes doubtful what is certain, and turns a very short time into a long one.

—St. Teresa of Avila

Virtue

The only true riches are those that make us rich in virtue.
Therefore, if you want to be rich, beloved, love true riches.
If you aspire to the heights of real honor, strive to reach the
kingdom of Heaven. If you value rank and renown, hasten
to be enrolled in the heavenly court of the Angels.

—*St. Gregory the Great*

The virtuous soul that is alone and without a master,
is like a lone burning coal; it will grow colder rather
than hotter.

—*St. John of the Cross*

Obey with humility your superiors, for obedience is the
backbone of faith. Be sympathetic to the weaknesses and
failings of others. Persevere in your holy vocation, to which
the Lord has so obviously called you. Keep in mind that
the crown of salvation is won only by those who persevere.
It is vain to begin a good action unless you bring it to full
completion. Maintain yourselves with holy emulation on the
path of virtue, which I have so ardently pursued, particularly
the practice of charity, humility, and patience.

—St. Francis of Paola, to his brothers

In a time of desolation, never forsake the good resolutions
you made in better times. Strive to remain patient—a virtue
contrary to the troubles that harass you—and remember that
you will be consoled.

—St. Ignatius of Loyola

In my long experience very often I had to be convinced of this great truth; that it is easier to become angry than to restrain oneself and easier to threaten a boy than to persuade him. Yes, it is more fitting to be persistent in punishing our own impatience and pride than to correct the boys. We must be firm but kind, and be patient with them.

—*St. John Bosco*

Patience is most perfect when it is least permeated by cares and worries. If the good Lord wishes to prolong the hour of trial, do not complain and look for the reason; but remember always, that the children of Israel had to remain forty years in the desert before reaching the Promised Land.

—*St. Padre Pio*

Patience is not good if when you may be free you allow yourself to become a slave.

—*St. Bernard*

There is no perfect virtue—none that bears fruit—unless it is exercised by means of our neighbor.

—St. Catherine of Siena

Certain virtues are greatly esteemed and always preferred by the general run of men because they are close at hand, easily noticed, and, in effect, material. Thus many people prefer bodily to spiritual alms, hair shirts, fasting, going barefoot, using the discipline, and physical mortifications to meekness, patience, modesty, and other mortifications of the heart although the latter are really higher virtues.

—St. Francis de Sales

Strive yourself to practice with great perfection the virtue opposite the fault that appears in her.

*—St. Teresa of Avila, on how to
deal with a difficult person*

Many appear full of mildness and sweetness as long as everything goes their own way; but the moment any contradiction or adversity arises, they are in a flame, and begin to rage like a burning mountain. Such people as these are like red-hot coals hidden under ashes. This is not the mildness which Our Lord undertook to teach us in order to make us like unto Himself.

—*St. Bernard*

Meekness, the greatest of virtues, is reckoned among the beatitudes. "Blessed are the meek, for they shall possess the land." For that blessed land, the heavenly Jerusalem, is not the spoil of warriors who have conquered, but the hoped-for inheritance of the meek, who patiently endure the evils of this life.

—*St. Basil the Great*

The practice of virtue became attractive, and seemed to come more naturally. At first, my face often betrayed my inward struggle, but little by little sacrifice, even at the first moment, became easier.

—*St. Thérèse of Lisieux*

In the case of the virtues, sir, it is very easy to pass from defect to excess, from being just to being rigorous and rashly zealous. It is said that good wine easily turns to vinegar, and that health in the highest degree is a sign of approaching illness.

—*St. Vincent de Paul*

Christ has made my soul beautiful with the jewels of grace and virtue. I belong to Him Whom the Angels serve.

—*St. Agnes*

Humility and Simplicity

There is more value in a little study of humility and in a single act of it than in all the knowledge in the world.

—*St. Teresa of Avila*

If you should ask me what are the ways of God, I would tell you that the first is humility, the second is humility, and the third is still humility. Not that there are no other precepts to give, but if humility does not precede all that we do, our efforts are fruitless.

—*St. Augustine*

True humility consists in not presuming on our own strength, but in trusting to obtain all things from the power of God.

—*St. Thomas Aquinas*

The gate of heaven is very low; only the humble can enter it.

—St. Elizabeth Ann Seton

The only way to make rapid progress along the path of divine love is to remain very little and put all our trust in Almighty God.

—St. Thérèse of Lisieux

Humility must always be doing its work like a bee making its honey in the hive: without humility all will be lost.

—St. Teresa of Avila

In all that you do, always be humble, guarding jealously the purity of your heart and the purity of your body; these are the two wings which will raise us to God and make us almost divine.

—St. Padre Pio

Little children follow and obey their father. They love their mother. They know nothing of covetousness, ill will, bad temper, arrogance and lying. This state of mind opens the road to heaven. To imitate our Lord's own humility, we must return to the simplicity of God's little ones.

—St. Hilary of Poitiers

God in His nature is most simple and cannot admit of any duplicity. If we then would be conformable to Him, we should try to become by virtue what He is by nature. We should be simple in our affections, intentions, actions, and words; we should do what we find to do without artifice or guile, making our exterior conformable to our interior. We should have no other object but God in our actions and seek to please Him alone in all things.

—St. Vincent de Paul

If you have fasted for two days, don't think yourself better than one who hasn't fasted. You fast and are peevish. The other eats and is pleasant. You work off your irritability and hunger by quarreling. The other eats and gives thanks to God.

—St. Jerome

Do nothing out of selfish ambition or vain conceit, but in humility consider others better than yourself.

—*St. Paul*

I have never wished for human glory, contempt it was that had attraction for my heart; but having recognized that this again was too glorious for me, I ardently desire to be forgotten.

—*St. Thérèse of Lisieux*

Satan fears and trembles before humble souls.

—*St. Padre Pio*

A humble person, if his opinion is asked, gives it in all simplicity and then leaves others to give theirs. Whether they are right or wrong, he says no more.

—*St. John Vianney*

A humble man is never hurried, hasty or perturbed, but at all times remains calm. Nothing can ever surprise, disturb or dismay him, for he suffers neither fear nor change in tribulations, neither surprise nor elation in enjoyment. All his joy and gladness are in what is pleasing to the Lord.

—St. Isaak of Syria

Then the Lord opened my mind and senses to the nature of my unbelief so that I may—however late—remember my sins and turn with all my heart to the Lord my God. He turned His attention to my abject humility and took pity on my youth and ignorance. He watched over me and protected me before I knew Him and before I was wise enough to distinguish between good and evil. He strengthened and comforted me as a father consoles a son.

—St. Patrick of Ireland

Jesus, the Lord, expects us to have the simplicity of a dove (see Mt 10:16). This means giving a straightforward opinion about things in the way we honestly see them, without needless reservations. It also means doing things without double-dealing or manipulation, our intention being focused solely on God. Each of us, then, should take care to behave always in the spirit of simplicity, remembering that God likes to deal with the simple, and that He conceals the secrets of heaven from the wise and prudent of this world and reveals them to little ones.

—*St. Vincent de Paul*

Keep a holy simplicity. Remain perfectly at peace, certain that God makes it His business to make you successful.

—*St. Raphaela Maria Porras*

Walk with simplicity on the road to the Lord, and don't torment your spirit. It is necessary to hate your faults, but do so tranquilly, not fastidiously and uneasily.

—*St. Padre Pio*

Charity

One must see God in everyone.

—St. Catherine Labouré

❦

Whatever you do, think not of yourselves but of God.

—St. Vincent Ferrer

❦

Miss no single opportunity of making some small sacrifice, here by a smiling look, there by a kindly word; always doing the smallest things right, and doing all for love.

—St. Thérèse of Lisieux

❦

Everything people leave after them in this world is lost, but for their charity and almsgiving they will receive a reward from God.

—*St. Francis of Assisi*

An egg given during life for love of God is more profitable for eternity than a cathedral full of gold given after death.

—*St. Albert the Great*

The bread you store up belongs to the hungry; the cloak that lies in your chest belongs to the naked; the gold you have hidden in the ground belongs to the poor.

—*St. Basil the Great*

God has no need of your money, but the poor have. You give it to the poor, and God receives it.

—*St. Augustine*

If you truly want to help the soul of your neighbor, you should approach God first with all your heart. Ask Him simply to fill you with charity, the greatest of all virtues; with it you can accomplish what you desire.

—*St. Vincent Ferrer*

It would be considered a theft on our part if we didn't give to someone in greater need than we are.

—*St. Francis of Assisi*

If a man wishes to take your coat, give him also whatever other articles of clothes you may have.

—*St. Augustine*

Many of the people who look forward to a long life put off doing good works, since they think that they will have plenty of time before they die. As for me, I prefer to be among those who consider that they have no time to lose if they wish to give God all the glory that they can before they die.

—*St. Margaret of Hungary*

All creatures have the same source as we have. Like us, they derive the life of thought, love, and will from the Creator. Not to hurt our humble brethren is our first duty to them; but to stop there is a complete misapprehension of the intentions of Providence. We have a higher mission. God wishes that we should succor them whenever they require it.

—St. Francis of Assisi

Do not grieve or complain that you were born in a time when you can no longer see God in the flesh. He did not in fact take this privilege from you. As He says: "Whatever you have done to the least of my brothers, you did to me."

—St. Augustine

I can't go to bed with a quiet conscience if during the day I've missed any chance, however slight, of preventing wrongdoing or of helping to bring about some good.

—St. Maria Crocifissa di Rosa

One single act done with aridity of spirit is worth more than many done with feelings of devotion.

—*St. Francis de Sales*

If something uncharitable is said in your presence, either speak in favor of the absent, or withdraw, or, if possible, stop the conversation.

—*St. John Vianney*

I cannot tolerate criticism and gossip in regard to our brothers. It is true that I sometimes enjoy teasing them, but grumbling makes me nauseous. We have so many faults to criticize in ourselves, why pick on our brothers? When we lack charity, we impair the roots of the tree of life, endangering its existence.

—*St. Padre Pio*

If we wish to keep peace with our neighbor, we should never remind anyone of his natural defects.

—*St. Philip Neri*

Remember that the Christian life is one of action; not of speech and daydreams.

—*St. Vincent Pallotti*

The word of God does not belong to him who hears or speaks it, but to him who puts it into practice.

—*St. Giles of Assisi*

Take O Lord, from our hearts all jealousy, indignation, wrath, and contention, and whatsoever may hurt charity and lesson brotherly love.

—*St. Thérèse of Lisieux*

True virtue has no limits, but goes on and on, and especially holy charity, which is the virtue of virtues, and which having a definite object, would become infinite if it could meet with a heart capable of infinity.

—*St. Francis de Sales*

Obedience

Obedience is a virtue of so excellent a nature, that Our Lord was pleased to mark its observance upon the whole course of His life; thus He often says, He did not come to do His Own will, but that of His Heavenly Father.

—St. Francis de Sales

We must conduct ourselves according to the purpose for which God made us, seeing that He made man to preside over all the things on earth and to be subject to Himself. Accordingly, we must rule and hold dominion over the things of the earth, but we must be subject to God by obeying and serving Him, and so we shall attain to the enjoyment of God.

—St. Thomas Aquinas

To do the will of God man must despise his own: the more he dies to himself, the more he will live to God.

—*St. Peter Claver*

I am quite resigned to live or to die, I am even willing to recover and go to Cochin-China if it is God's will.

—*St. Thérèse of Lisieux*

A little drop of simple obedience is worth a million times more than a whole vase of the choicest contemplation.

—*St. Mary Magdalen de´ Pazzi*

By obedience knowledge is increased.

—*St. Thomas Aquinas*

Be content to obey, which is never a small thing for the soul who has chosen God as his portion, and resign yourself to be for now a small hive bee able to make honey.

—*St. Padre Pio*

Take a corpse and bring it where thou wilt! It makes no resistance, does not change its attitude, does not wish to move. If thou placest it on a throne, it looks down and not up; if thou dressest it in purple, it appears only paler than before. It is so with the really obedient; he never asks whither he is sent, he never is concerned as to how he came here, does not seek to be taken away. If he acquires honors, they only increase his humility, and the more he is praised, the more unworthy does he consider himself.

—*St. Francis of Assisi, in response*
to his Brothers' question of how
to be perfectly obedient

For the superior is not to be obeyed because he is prudent, or kind, or divinely gifted in any other way, but for the sole reason that he holds the place of God and exercises the authority of Him Who says, "He who hears you hears me and he who despises you despises me."

—*St. Ignatius of Loyola*

If you begin to grieve at this, to judge your superior, to murmur in your heart, even though you outwardly fulfill what is commanded, this is not the virtue of obedience, but a cloak over your malice.

—*St. Bernard of Clairvaux*

The pleasure which a man seeks in the gratification of his own inclinations is quickly changed into bitterness, and leaves nothing behind but the regret of having been ignorant of the secret of true beatitude and of the way of the saints.

—*St. Isidore of Seville*

"Thy will be done!"—What a comfort and support those four little words are to my soul. I have repeated them until they are softened to the sweetest harmony.

—*St. Elizabeth Ann Seton*

Entire conformity and resignation to the divine will is truly a road on which we cannot go wrong, and it is the only road that leads us to taste and enjoy that peace which sensual and earthly men know nothing of.

—*St. Philip Neri*

Obedience is the only virtue that implants the other virtues in the heart and preserves them after they have been so implanted.

—*St. Gregory the Great*

At all times, try to conform to the will of God in everything that you do, and have no fear. This conformity is the surest way to Heaven.

—*St. Padre Pio*

Peace and Joy

Do not look forward to what may happen tomorrow. The same Everlasting Father, who takes care of you today, will take care of you tomorrow. He will either shield you from suffering, or give you unfailing strength to bear it. Be at peace then, and put aside all anxious thoughts and imaginations.

—St. Francis de Sales

Tolerance is the bond of all friendship, and unites people in heart and opinion and action, not only with each other, but in unity with our Lord, so that they may really be at peace.

—St. Vincent de Paul

In the last few months one has often heard the complaint that the many prayers for peace are still without effect. What right have we to be heard? Our desire for peace is undoubtedly genuine and sincere. But does it come from a completely purified heart?

—St. Edith Stein

We have been called to heal wounds, to unite what has fallen apart, and to bring home those who have lost their way.

—St. Francis of Assisi

Be courageous, do not be cast down. Trust in God and hope that He will grant you every grace. Do not rely on yourself, but rather on the Lord, and if you imagine that all is calm, then be assured that the enemy is quite near. Do not put too much confidence in peace, for in the midst of rest war may break out.

—St. Gerard Majella

Seek to keep peace. Protect widows and orphans as you have done before. Such care gives the greatest joy possible on earth since it is thanksgiving to God, and it gives God greater joy in heaven. You must also prevent public sins and always personally insist on justice. You should carry the passion of God in your hearts, for it will be your consolation in your last hour.

—*St. Nicholas of Flue*

The soul of one who loves God always swims in joy, always keeps holiday, and is always in a mood for singing.

—*St. John of the Cross*

Melancholy is the poison of devotion. When one is in tribulation, it is necessary to be more happy and more joyful because one is nearer to God.

—*St. Clare of Assisi*

Leave sadness to those in the world. We who work for God should be lighthearted.

—*St. Leonard of Port Maurice*

Why, dearest daughter, do you waste time in sadness when time is so precious for the salvation of poor sinners? Get rid of your melancholy immediately. Don't think any more about yourself. Do not indulge in so many useless and dangerous reflections. Look ahead always without ever looking back. Keep your gaze fixed on the summit of perfection where Christ awaits you. He wants you despoiled of all things, intent only on procuring His greater glory during this brief time of your existence. For the short time that remains, is it worthwhile to lose yourself in melancholy like those who think only of themselves, as if all were to end with this life? . . . Carry your cross then but carry it joyfully, my daughter. Think that Jesus loves you very much. And in return for such love, don't lose yourself in so many desires, but accept daily with serenity whatever comes your way.

*—St. Frances Xavier Cabrini, in a
letter to one of her sisters*

The safest remedy against the thousand snares and wiles of the enemy is spiritual joy.

—St. Francis of Assisi

Jesus is honey in the mouth, music in the ear and a shout of joy in the heart.

—*St. Bernard of Clairvaux*

Let your understanding strengthen your patience. In serenity look forward to the joy that follows sadness.

—*St. Peter Damian*

It is always springtime in the heart that loves God.

—*St. John Vianney*

Rejoice and be glad always, for you shall not be put to shame.

—*St. Boniface*

Human Nature

Men go abroad to wonder at the height of mountains, at the huge waves of the sea, at the long courses of the rivers, at the vast compass of the ocean, at the circular motion of the stars, and they pass by themselves without wondering.

—*St. Augustine*

He who never meditates, is like a person who never looks in the mirror; therefore, not knowing that he is untidy, he goes out looking disorderly. The person who meditates and directs his thoughts to God, Who is the mirror of his soul, tries to know his faults, attempts to correct them, moderates his impulses, and puts his conscience in order.

—*St. Padre Pio*

Between the spirit and the flesh there is a continual combat.
Now, if you wish the spirit to win, you must assist it by prayer
and resist the flesh by such means as fasting (for by fasting the
flesh is weakened.)

—St. Thomas Aquinas

Our body is like a jackass that must be beaten, but just a little,
otherwise it will throw us to the ground, and refuse to carry us.

—St. Padre Pio

We all talk of reforming others without ever reforming
ourselves.

—St. Peter of Alcántara

Human nature grows tired of always doing the same thing,
and it is God's will that this [is] because of the opportunity of
practicing two great virtues. The first is perseverance, which
will bring us to our goal. The other is steadfastness, which
overcomes the difficulties on the way.

—St. Vincent de Paul

Raise up your heart after a fall, sweetly and gently, humbling yourself before God in the knowledge of your misery, and do not be astonished at your weakness, since it is not surprising that weakness should be weak, infirmity infirm, and frailty frail.

—St. Francis de Sales

O soul pressed down by the corruptible body, and weighed down by earthly thoughts, many and various; behold and see, if thou canst, that God is truth.

—St. Augustine

Now true and lasting friendship require certain dispositions; those of our Lord, we know, are absolutely perfect; our, vicious, sensual, and thankless; and you cannot, therefore, bring yourselves to love Him as He loves you because you have not the disposition to do so.

—St. Teresa of Avila

If I had to advise parents, I should tell them to take great care about the people with whom their children associate . . . Much harm may result from bad company, and we are inclined by nature to follow what is worse than what is better.

—*St. Elizabeth Ann Seton*

Vice is contrary to man's nature, in as much as he is a rational animal: and when a thing acts contrary to its nature, that which is natural to it is corrupted little by little.

—*St. Thomas Aquinas*

Look at me. God's mercy has preserved me to this day in bodily virginity, but I confess that I have not escaped from the imperfection of being more excited by the conversation of young women than by being talked at by an old woman.

—*St. Dominic*

God is like a mother who carries her child in her arms by the edge of a precipice. While she is seeking all the time to keep him from danger, he is doing his best to get into it.

—*St. John Vianney*

As long as there remains a drop of blood in our body, there will be a struggle between right and wrong.

—*St. Padre Pio*

We are encouraged to keep our souls pure, because our nature was ennobled and raised through being united to God, to the extent of being assumed into union with a divine Person.

—*St. Thomas Aquinas*

The Material World and Poverty

The love of money is a root of all kinds of evil.

—*St. Paul*

Lust for riches, properly speaking, brings darkness on the soul, when it puts out the light of charity, by preferring the love of riches to the love of God.

—*St. Thomas Aquinas*

Riches are the instrument of all vices, because they render us capable of putting even our worst desires into execution.

—*St. Ambrose of Milan*

A strong, resolute soul can live in the world without being infected by any of its moods, find sweet springs of piety amid its salty waves, and fly through flames of earthly lusts without burning the wings of its holy desires for a devout life.

—*St. Francis de Sales*

We ought to love what Christ loved on earth, and to set no store by those things which He regarded as of no account.

—*St. John Vianney*

When the soul is troubled, lonely and darkened, then it turns easily to the outer comfort and to the empty enjoyments of the world.

—*St. Francis of Assisi*

There are some who are never satisfied with what they have and always want more. This is lack of moderation, since desire should always be measured according to one's needs: "Give me neither beggary nor riches; give me but the necessities of life."

—*St. Thomas Aquinas*

Oh how divided in aim are the hearts of men! Some enjoy the wealth they have gained, others love riches but never have any to enjoy.

—St. Elfleda of Whitby

Be not anxious about what you have, but about what you are.

—St. Gregory the Great

Quietly to trust in God is better than trying to safeguard material interests. I learned that from bitter experience.

—St. Emilie de Vialar

He made man for a certain purpose; but not for the sake of material pleasures, since dumb animals have them, but that he may have eternal life. For it is the Lord's will that man have eternal life.

—St. Thomas Aquinas

For those in the married state, the best example we can cite is that of St. Joachim and St. Anne, who every year divided their income into three equal parts. One was for the poor, the second for the temple and the divine service, and the third for themselves.

—St. Ignatius of Loyola

The more we indulge ourselves in soft living and pampered bodies, the more rebellious they will become against the spirit.

—St. Rita of Cascia

Perfection does not consist in not seeing the world, but in not having a taste or relish for it.

—St. Francis de Sales

Poverty is true riches. So precious is poverty that God's Only-Begotten Son came on earth in search of it. In heaven He had superabundance of all goods. Nothing was lacking there but poverty.

—St. Anthony of Padua

None need be fearful of poverty who have acquired the riches of wisdom.

—St. Thomas Aquinas

Receive from the hand of God poverty as cheerfully as riches, hunger and want as plenty, and you will conquer the devil and subdue all your passions.

—St. Macarius

If everyone would take only according to his needs and would leave the surplus to the needy, no one would be rich, no one poor, no one in misery.

—St. Basil the Great

Poverty is a remover of cares and the mother of holiness.

—St. Meriadoc

Poverty is an easy way to God. Poverty is the mother of humility. It is as difficult to preserve humility amid riches as purity in the midst of delights and luxury. Poverty sets free. When a person delights in and gloats over his possessions, in reality he limits, even loses his freedom. The mania of riches has enslaved him. He is lowered in status, being no longer the owner but the owned. He has subordinated himself to his goods. Such servile subjection becomes evident in the fever that dominates him and the anguish that racks him when he loses some of his possessions. In short, true liberty is not found except in voluntary poverty.

—*St. Anthony of Padua*

If we had any possessions we should be forced to have arms to protect them, since possessions are a cause of disputes and strife, and in many ways we should be hindered from loving God and our neighbor. Therefore, in this life, we wish to have no temporal possessions.

—*St. Francis of Assisi*

Sin and Forgiveness

Our own evil inclinations are far more dangerous than any
external enemies.

—St. Ambrose of Milan

It is better not to allow anger, however just and reasonable,
to enter at all, than to admit it in ever so slight a degree; once
admitted, it will not be easily expelled, for, though at first but
a small plant, it will immediately grow into a large tree.

—St. Augustine

When you feel the assaults of passion and anger, then is the
time to be silent. Jesus was silent in the midst of His ignominies
and sufferings. O holy silence, rich in great virtues! O holy
silence, which is a key of gold, keeping in safety the great
treasure of holy virtues!

—St. Paul of the Cross

Anger is a kind of temporary madness.

—St. Basil the Great

Pride makes us hate our equals because they are our equals;
our inferiors from fear that they may equal us; our superiors
because they are above us.

—St. John Vianney

Out of a forward will lust had sprung; and lust pampered had
become custom; and custom indulged had become necessity.
These were the links of the chain; this is the bondage in which
I was bound.

—St. Augustine

Fear is a greater evil than evil itself.

—St. Francis de Sales

When we converse with slanderers and laugh with them, when we delight in these frivolities and other faults of the same order, what do we do, if not confirm that evil things do not displease us?

—St. Thomas Aquinas

Drunkenness is the ruin of reason. It is premature old age. It is temporary death.

—St. Basil the Great

Nothing is more foolish than for man, who ought in this present life so to work that he may live eternally, to live idly. . . . From idleness evil is learned, as from a bad master.

—St. Thomas Aquinas

There is still time for endurance, time for patience, time for healing, time for change. Have you slipped? Rise up. Have you sinned? Cease. Do not stand among sinners, but leap aside. For when you turn away and weep, then you will be saved.

—St. Basil the Great

The Church teaches us that mercy belongs to God. Let us implore Him to bestow on us the spirit of mercy and compassion, so that we are filled with it and my never lose it. Only consider how much we ourselves are in need of mercy.

—*St. Vincent de Paul*

You should bear patiently the bad temper of other people, the slights, the rudeness that may be offered you.

—*St. John Bosco*

Pardon one another so that later on you will not remember the injury. The recollection of an injury is in itself wrong. It adds to our anger, nurtures our sin and hates what is good. It is a rusty arrow and poison for the soul. It puts all virtue to flight.

—*St. Francis of Paola*

Penance is the purifier of the soul.

—*St. Elizabeth Ann Seton*

I believe very few souls are so perfect in the beginning. We would be happy enough if they managed not to fall into these imperfections of pride. . . . God places these souls in the dark night so as to purify them of these imperfections and make them advance.

—*St. John of the Cross*

Remember: The sinner who is sorry for his sins, is closer to God than the just man who boasts of his good works.

—*St. Padre Pio*

Confession heals, confession justifies, confession grants pardon of sin, all hope consists in confession; in confession there is a chance for mercy.

—*St. Isidore of Seville*

Go to your confessor; open your heart to him; display to him all the recesses of your soul; take the advice that he will give you with the utmost humility and simplicity. For God, Who has an infinite love for obedience, frequently renders profitable the counsels we take from others, but especially from those who are the guides of our souls.

—*St. Francis de Sales*

The penances done by some persons are as carefully ordered as their lives. They observe great discretion in their penances, lest they should injure their health. You need never fear that they will kill themselves; they are eminently reasonable folk! Their love is not yet ardent enough to overwhelm their reason.

—*St. Teresa of Avila*

Sinners are led back to God by holy meekness better than by cruel scolding.

—*St. Francis of Assisi*

You can win more converts with a spoonful of honey than with a barrelful of vinegar.

—*St. Francis de Sales*

Nothing is sweeter than the calm of conscience: nothing safer than the purity of soul, which yet no one can bestow on itself because it is properly the gift of another.

—*St. Columban*

Knowledge and Intellect

Jesus needs neither books nor Doctors of Divinity in order to instruct souls; He, the Doctor of Doctors, He teaches without noise of words.

—St. Thérèse of Lisieux

Human reason is very deficient in things concerning God. A sign of this is that philosophers in their researches, by natural investigation, into human affairs, have fallen into many errors, and have disagreed among themselves. . . . It was necessary for Divine matters to be delivered to them by way of faith, being told to them, as it were, by God Himself Who cannot lie.

—St. Thomas Aquinas

True wisdom, then, consists in works, not in great talents, which the world admires; for the wise in the world's estimation . . . are the foolish who set at naught the will of God, and know not how to control their passions.

—St. Brigit of Sweden

Better to illuminate than merely to shine, to deliver to others contemplated truths than merely to contemplate.

—St. Thomas Aquinas

Occupy your minds with good thoughts, or the enemy will find the bad ones. Unoccupied they cannot be.

—St. Thomas More

This intellect is so wild that it doesn't seem to be anything else than a frantic madman no one can tie down.

—St. Teresa of Avila

My Brothers, my Brothers, the Lord called me to travel the paths of humility and simplicity and with me all those who want to follow and copy me. Do not then speak to me either of the Rule of St. Benedict or of St. Augustine or of St. Bernard or of any other. For the Lord said to me, that He wished me to be a fool and a simpleton, the like of which was never seen before, and that He wished to bring us on another road than that of wisdom. But God wants to put you all to shame with your wisdom and knowledge, and I expect that He will send His master of discipline and punish you, so that whether you will or not you must with shame turn back to your place.

—*St. Francis of Assisi*

Poor human reason when it trusts in itself substitutes the strangest absurdities for the highest divine concepts.

—*St. John Chrysostom*

No matter how enlightened one may be through natural and acquired knowledge, he cannot enter into himself to delight in the Lord unless Christ be his mediator.

—*St. Bonaventure*

Learning unsupported by grace may get into our ears; it never reaches the heart. But when God's grace touches our innermost minds to bring understanding, His word which has been received by the ear sinks deep into the heart.

—*St. Isidore of Seville*

The good of reason flourishes more in the temperate man.

—*St. Thomas Aquinas*

Never read books you aren't sure about . . . even supposing that these bad books are very well written from a literary point of view. Let me ask you this: Would you drink something you knew was poisoned just because it was offered to you in a golden cup?

—*St. John Bosco*

Remember that a mother holds a baby when teaching him how to take his first steps; but later, the child must walk by himself. You, therefore, must think with your own head.

—*St. Padre Pio*

No one draws closer to a knowledge of the truth than he who has advanced far in the knowledge of divine things, and yet knows that something always remains for him to seek.

—*St. Leo the Great*

Suffering and Death

Christ tells us that if we wish to join Him, we shall travel the way He took. It is surely not right that the Son of God should go His way on the path of shame while the sons of men walk the way of worldly honor.

—St. John of Avila

I would willingly endure all the sufferings of this world to be raised a degree higher in Heaven, and to possess the smallest increase of the knowledge of God's greatness.

—St. Teresa of Avila

I have had crosses in plenty—more than I could carry, almost. I set myself to ask for the love of crosses—then I was happy.

—St. John Vianney

For one pain endured with joy, we shall love the good God more forever.

—St. Thérèse of Lisieux

I hope that I so blessed will be
That every suffering pleases me.

—St. Francis of Assisi

This is not a country for solitude and silence, but for warfare and crucifixion. You are not to stay in his silent agonies of the Garden at night, but go from post to pillar, to the very fastening of the Cross. If you suffer so much the better for our high journey above.

—St. Elizabeth Ann Seton

The debt we pay for this beautiful creation and the many enjoyments of this life are to be borne in some degree by us all. Human life and sorrow are inseparable.

—St. Elizabeth Ann Seton

The more we are afflicted in this world, the greater is our assurance in the next; the more sorrow in the present, the greater will be our joy in the future.

—St. Isidore of Seville

In the middle of my physical sufferings, the inner music of my soul will not stop praising God with acts of virtue offering Him my love.

—St. Genoveva Torres Morales

Many would be willing to have afflictions provided that they not be inconvenienced by them.

—St. Francis de Sales

Whenever anything disagreeable or displeasing happens to you, remember Christ crucified and be silent.

—St. John of the Cross

Have patience, for the sickness of the body is given to us by God for the salvation of our soul; for sickness is of great merit when it is endured in peace.

—*St. Francis of Assisi*

Contradictions, sickness, scruples, spiritual aridity, and all the inner and outward torments are the chisel with which God carves His statues for paradise.

—*St. Alphonsus Liguori*

When men wish for old age for themselves, what else do they wish for but lengthened infirmity.

—*St. Augustine*

We will lie down for such a long time after death that it is worthwhile to keep standing while we are alive. Let us work now; one day we will rest.

—*St. Agostina Pietrantoni*

My Good Shepherd, who have shown Your very gentle mercy to us unworthy sinners in various physical pains and sufferings, give grace and strength to me, Your little lamb, that in no tribulation or anguish or pain may I turn away from You.

—*St. Francis of Assisi*

He who bears his sufferings with patience for God's sake, will soon arrive at high perfection. He will be master of the world and will already have one foot in the other world.

—*St. Giles of Assisi*

Death is no more than falling blindly into the arms of God.

—*St. María Maravillas de Jesús*

After my death, I will let fall a shower of roses. I will spend my heaven doing good upon earth. I will raise up a mighty host of little saints. My mission is to make God loved.

—*St. Thérèse of Lisieux*

Live so as not to fear death. For those who live well in the world, death is not frightening but sweet and precious.

—*St. Rose of Viterbo*

I feel certain that my mission will not come to an end upon my death, but will begin. O doubting souls, I will draw aside for you the veils of heaven to convince you of God's goodness, so that you will no longer continue to wound with your distrust the sweetest Heart of Jesus. God is Love and Mercy.

—*St. Faustina*

Go forth in peace, for you have followed the good road. Go forth without fear, for He that created you has sanctified you, has always protected you, and loves you as a mother. Blessed be Thou, O God, for having created me.

—St. Clare of Assisi,
speaking to herself on her deathbed

They must be esteemed to have lost their sense, who either pursuing abundance, or fearing lack of temporal goods, lose those which are eternal.

—St. Thomas Aquinas

Our labor here is brief, but the reward is eternal. Do not be disturbed by the clamor of the world, which passes like a shadow. Do not let the false delights of a deceptive world deceive you.

—St. Clare of Assisi

The end of my labors has come. All that I have written
appears to me as so much straw after the things that have
been revealed to me.

—St. Thomas Aquinas

I never experienced so keenly the presence of this beloved
Lord as I have since I have been ill. It is as if I were seeing the
good Jesus, Him and His holy Mother, here, continually seated
at my side, under a visible form, to console me, cheer me, and
to encourage me throughout all the hours of my long and
painful suffering.

—St. Elizabeth Ann Seton

Christ's martyrs feared neither death nor pain. He triumphed
in them who lived in them; and they, who lived not for
themselves but for Him, found in death itself the way to life.

—St. Augustine

For I trust, in whatever manner I die, that I shall not be deprived of the mercy of my God, without which my eternal ruin would be inevitable, whether I die an unprepared death, or whether I have long anticipated my end.

—*St. Gertrude the Great*

A man may very well lose his head and yet come to no harm— yea, I say to unspeakable good and everlasting happiness.

—*St. Thomas More*

Sainthood

If they, why not I?—If these men and women could become saints, why cannot I with the help of Him who is all-powerful?

—St. Augustine

What saint has ever won his crown without first contending for it?

—St. Jerome

Do not worry about the mockery of fools. Remember that the Saints, who always scorned the world and the mundane, have thwarted the world and its maxims.

—St. Padre Pio

The saints live not after the fashion of the world. . . . The dignity of the saints is so great because they are not of this world, but "of the household of God."

—*St. Thomas Aquinas*

It is not those who commit the least faults who are most holy, but those who have the greatest courage, the greatest generosity, the greatest love, who make the boldest efforts to overcome themselves, and are not immoderately apprehensive of tripping.

—*St. Francis de Sales*

After seven years in the religious life, I still am weak and imperfect. I always feel, however, the same bold confidence of becoming a great saint because I don't count on my merits since I have none, but I trust in Him who is Virtue and Holiness.

—*St. Thérèse of Lisieux*

One should not wish to become a saint in four days but step by step.

—*St. Philip Neri*

No, I'm not a saint; I've never performed the actions of a saint. I'm a very little soul upon whom God has bestowed graces; that's what I am. What I say is the truth; you'll see this in heaven.

—*St. Thérèse of Lisieux, said*
toward the end of her life

It is better to err by excess of mercy than by excess of severity. . . . Wilt thou become a Saint? Be severe to thyself but kind to others.

—*St. John Chrysostom*

If being a saint consists in having no taste and a strong stomach, I admit I may be one.

—*St. Peter Claver*

A saint was once asked, while playing happily with his companions, what he would do if an angel told him that in a quarter of an hour he would die and have to appear before the judgment seat of God. The saint promptly replied that he would continue playing because I am certain these games are pleasing to God.

—St. John Bosco

Let us become saints so that after having been together on earth, we may be together in Heaven.

—St. Padre Pio

The greater the charity of the Saints in their heavenly home, the more they intercede for those who are still on their journey and the more they can help them by their prayers; the more they are united with God, the more effective those prayers are. This is in accordance with Divine order, which makes higher things react upon lower things, like the brightness of the sun filling the atmosphere.

—St. Thomas Aquinas

It is difficult to become a saint. Difficult, but not impossible. The road to perfection is long, as long as one's lifetime. Along the way, consolation becomes rest; but as soon as your strength is restored, you must diligently get up and resume the trip.

—St. Padre Pio

Words of Wisdom

Think well. Speak well. Do well. These three things, through the mercy of God, will make a man go to heaven.

—*St. Camillus de Lellis*

❧

Here is a rule for everyday life: Do not do anything which you cannot offer to God.

—*St. John Vianney*

❧

No one heals himself by wounding another.

—*St. Ambrose of Milan*

❧

Pay no attention to the affairs of others, whether they be good or bad, for besides the danger of sin, this is a cause of distractions and lack of spirit.

—*St. John of the Cross*

Beware not to disturb yourself, nor to be irritated on account of the defects of others, for it would be folly, because you saw a man throw himself into a pit, to throw yourself into another.

—*St. Bonaventure*

The gifts of grace increase as the struggles increase.

—*St. Rose of Lima*

The principal act of courage is to endure and withstand dangers doggedly rather than to attack them.

—*St. Thomas Aquinas*

A person who governs his passions is master of the world. We must either rule them, or be ruled by them. It is better to be the hammer than the anvil.

—*St. Dominic*

Sorrow can be alleviated by good sleep, a bath, and a glass of wine.

—*St. Thomas Aquinas*

Don't spend your energies on things that generate worry, anxiety and anguish. Only one thing is necessary: Lift up your spirit, and love God.

—*St. Padre Pio*

Prayers of the Saints

Let nothing worry you;
Nothing dismay you;
Everything passes;
God does not change.
If you have patience
You can do anything.
Those who have God
Want for nothing;
God alone is enough.

—*St. Teresa of Avila*

O Jesus, keep me under the standard of your cross. Let me not just look at you crucified but have you living in my heart.

—*St. Bernadette*

Almighty, eternal, just and merciful God, grant us in our misery that we may do for your sake alone what we know you want us to do, and always want what pleases you; so that, cleansed and enlightened interiorly and fired with the ardor of the Holy Spirit, we may be able to follow in the footsteps of your Son, our Lord Jesus Christ, and so make our way to you.

—St. Francis of Assisi

Christ shield me this day: Christ with me, Christ before me, Christ behind me, Christ in me, Christ beneath me, Christ above me, Christ on my right, Christ on my left, Christ when I lie down, Christ when I arise, Christ in the heart of every person who thinks of me, Christ in every eye that sees me, Christ in the ear that hears me.

—St. Patrick of Ireland, from his breastplate

O my God! Teach me to be generous; to give and not to count the cost; to fight and not to heed the wounds; to toil and not to seek for rest; to labor and not to seek for any reward save that of doing your blessed will.

—St. Ignatius of Loyola

Lord, make me an instrument of your peace.
Where there is hatred, let me sow love.
Where there is injury, pardon.
Where there is doubt, faith.
Where there is despair, hope.
Where there is darkness, light.
Where there is sadness, joy.

O Divine Master, grant that I may not so much seek
to be consoled, as to console;
to be understood, as to understand;
to be loved, as to love;
for it is in giving that we receive,
it is in pardoning that we are pardoned,
it is in dying that we are born to eternal life.

—St. Francis of Assisi

Oh my Jesus, give me Your strength when my weak nature rebels against the distress and suffering of this life of exile, and enable me to accept everything with serenity and peace. With my whole strength I cling to Your merits, Your sufferings, Your expiation, and Your tears, so that I may be able to cooperate with You in the work of salvation. Give me strength to fly from sin, the only cause of Your agony, Your sweat of blood, and Your death. Destroy in me all that displeases You and fill my heart with the fire of Your holy love and all Your sufferings. Clasp me tenderly, firmly, close to You that I may never leave You alone in Your cruel Passion. I ask only for a place of rest in Your Heart. My desire is to share in Your agony and be beside You in the Garden. May my soul be inebriated by Your love and fed with the bread of Your sorrow. Amen.

—*St. Padre Pio*

Grant to me, O Lord my God, that I may not falter in times of prosperity or adversity, so that I may not be exalted in the former, nor dejected in the latter.

—*St. Thomas Aquinas*

Jesus Christ my God, I adore you and I thank you for all the graces you have given me this day. I offer you my sleep and all the moments of this night, and I implore you to keep me safe from sin. To this end I place myself in your sacred side and under the mantle of our Lady, my Mother. Let your holy angels surround me and keep me in peace; and let your blessing be upon me. Amen.

—*St. Alphonsus de Liguori*

God our Father, you who exhort us to pray to you and give us what has been asked of you, listen to me, who am shivering in this darkness, and stretch out your hand to me. Let me see your light. Bring me back from errors and bring it about that under your guidance I may return again to myself and to you.

—*St. Augustine*

Listing of Quoted Saints

St. Agnes (291–304) — Martyr. Patron of Girl Scouts, virgins.

St. Agostina Pietrantoni (1864–1894) — Nurse and Martyr. Patron of abuse victims, the impoverished.

St. Albert the Great (1206–1280) — Natural Scientist, Bishop, and Doctor of the Church.[1] Patron of medical technologists, science students, scientists.

St. Alphonsus Liguori (1696–1787) — Lawyer, Bishop, and Doctor of the Church. Patron of confessors, moral theologians.

St. Ambrose of Milan (340–397) — Bishop and Doctor of the Church. Patron of bees, beekeepers, candlemakers.

St. Anselm of Canterbury (1033–1109) — Bishop and Doctor of the Church.

St. Anthony Mary Claret (1807–1870) — Missionary and Bishop. Patron of savings banks, weavers.

St. Anthony of Padua (1195–1231) — Franciscan and Doctor of the Church. Patron of the illiterate, the poor, Portugal, pregnant women, sterile women, invoked to find lost objects.

St. Augustine (354–430) — Bishop and Doctor of the Church. Patron of printers, theologians.

St. Basil the Great (329–379) — Bishop and Doctor of the Church. Patron of hospital administrators, poets, Russia.

St. Benedict Joseph Labre (1748–1783) — Impoverished preacher. Patron of beggars, the homeless.

St. Bernadette (1844–1879) — Religious.[2] Patron of shepherds.

St. Bernard (778–842) — Bishop. Patron of agricultural laborers.

St. Bernard of Clairvaux (1090–1153) — Abbot and Doctor of the Church. Patron of beekeepers, candlemakers, skiers.

St. Bonaventure (1221–1274) — Bishop, Cardinal, and Doctor of the Church. Patron of theologians, messengers, porters, weavers.

St. Boniface (680–754) — Bishop and martyr. Patron of Germany.

St. Brigit of Sweden (1303–1373) — Founder[3] and Queen. Patron of Sweden.

St. Camillus de Lellis (1559–1614) — Founder. Patron of hospitals, nurses, the sick.

St. Catherine Labouré (1806–1870) — Religious. Her series of visions led to the Miraculous Medal.

St. Catherine of Siena (1347–1380) — Doctor of the Church. Patron of Italy.

St. Clare of Assisi (1194–1253) — Founder. Patron of the blind, embroiderers, television.

St. Columban (c. 543–615) — Abbot and Missionary. Patron of Ireland.

St. Dominic (c. 1170–1221) — Founder. Protector of astronomers, orators, seamstresses.

St. Edith Stein (1891–1942) — Religious and Martyr. Patron of Europe.

St. Edmund the Martyr (841–870) — King and Martyr.

St. Elfleda of Whitby (653–714) — Abbess.

St. Elizabeth Ann Seton (1774–1821) — Founder and first American-born saint.

St. Emilie de Vialar (1797–1856) — Founder.

St. Faustina (1905–1938) — Religious. Patron of the city of Brescia.

St. Fidelis of Sigmaringen (1577–1622) — Priest and Martyr.

St. Frances Xavier Cabrini (1850–1917) — Founder and first American citizen to be canonized. Patron of emigrants, immigrants, hospital administrators.

St. Francis de Sales (1567–1622) — Bishop and Doctor of the Church. Patron of editors, journalists, writers.

St. Francis of Assisi (1181–1226) — Founder. Patron of ecologists, florists, Italy, merchants, poets.

St. Francis of Paola (1416–1507) — Founder. Patron of hermits, seafarers.

St. Genoveva Torres Morales (1870–1956) — Founder.

St. Gerard Majella (1726–1755) — Redemptorist lay brother. Patron of childbirth, mothers, pregnant women.

St. Gertrude the Great (1256–1302) — Nun. Patron of the West Indies.

St. Giles of Assisi (d. 1262) — early Franciscan. Patron of the disabled, the homeless.

St. Gregory of Nyssa (c. 330–395) — Bishop.

St. Gregory the Great (c. 540–604) — Pope and Doctor of the Church. Patron of music, Popes, scholars, schoolchildren, singers, teachers.

St. Hilary of Poitiers (c. 315–367) — Bishop and Doctor of the Church. Patron of lawyers.

St. Ignatius of Loyola (1491–1556) — Founder. Patron of Jesuits, soldiers.

St. Irenaeus (c. 130–c. 208) — Bishop.

St. Isaak of Syria (7th century) — Bishop.

St. Isidore of Seville (c. 560–636) — Bishop and Doctor of the Church. Patron of Spain.

St. Jean-Baptiste de La Salle (1651–1719) — Founder. Patron of teachers.

St. Jerome (c. 342–420) — Doctor of the Church. Patron of book sellers, librarians, students, translators.

St. Joaquina (1783–1854) — Widow and Founder. Patron of abuse victims, exiles, widows.

St. John Bosco (1815–1888) — Founder. Patron of apprentices, editors, educators, students.

St. John Chrysostom (c. 347–407) — Bishop and Doctor of the Church. Patron of exiles, orators, preachers.

St. John of Avila (1499–1569) — Priest and spiritual advisor to number of saints including St. Teresa of Avila and St. John of the Cross. Patron of Andalusia, Spain.

St. John of the Cross (1542–1591) — Carmelite and Doctor of the Church. Patron of mystics, theologians, poets.

St. John Vianney (1786–1859) — Parish priest. Patron of parish priests.

St. Joseph Cafasso (1811–1860) — Priest. Patron of prisoners.

St. Leo the Great (d. 461) — Pope and Doctor of the Church. Patron of choirs, musicians, singers.

St. Leonard of Port Maurice (1676–1751) — Franciscan friar.

St. Macarius (300–391) — Egyptian monk.

St. Margaret of Hungary (1242–1270) — Princess and Nun. Invoked against floods.

St. Maria Crocifissa di Rosa (1813–1855) — Founder.

St. María Maravillas de Jesús (1891–1974) — Carmelite Nun and Founder.

St. Mary Euphrasia Pelletier (1796–1868) — Founder.

St. Mary Magdalen de' Pazzi (1566–1607) — Carmelite Nun. Patron of Florence, Naples.

St. Meriadoc (4th century) — Bishop. Invoked against deafness.

St. Nicholas of Flue (1417–1487) — Hermit. Patron of Switzerland.

St. Padre Pio (1887–1968) — Capuchin friar.

St. Patrick of Ireland (387–493) — Bishop. Patron of Ireland, Nigeria, miners, invoked against snakes.

St. Paul (3–65) — Apostle and Martyr. Patron of Greece, Malta, rope makers, tent makers.

St. Paul of the Cross (1694–1775) — Founder.

St. Peter Claver (1580–1654) — Missionary. Patron of African-Americans, Colombia, slaves.

St. Peter Damian (1001–1072) — Hermit, Bishop, and Doctor of the Church. Invoked against headaches.

St. Peter of Alcántara (1499–1562) — Franciscan reformer. Patron of nightwatchmen.

St. Philip Neri (1515–1595) — Founder. Patron of Rome.

St. Raphaela Maria Porras (1850–1925) — Founder.

St. Rita of Cascia (c. 1381–1457) — Widow and Nun. Patron of desperate cases, the unhappily married, invoked against infertility.

St. Rose of Lima (1586–1617) — Dominican tertiary. Patron of florists, gardeners, South America.

St. Rose of Viterbo (1233–1251) — Secular Franciscan. Patron of exiles, florists.

St. Teresa of Avila (1515–1582) — Founder and Doctor of the Church. Patron of lace makers, Spain, invoked against headaches.

St. Teresa of the Andes (1900–1920) — Teresian Carmelite.

St. Thérèse of Lisieux (1873–1897) — Carmelite nun and Doctor of the Church. Patron of France, missions, pilots, invoked against tuberculosis.

St. Thomas Aquinas (1225–1274) — Religious and Doctor of the Church. Patron of academics, booksellers, Catholic universities, colleges, schools.

St. Thomas More (1478–1535) — Martyr. Patron saint of civil servants, lawyers, politicians.

St. Vincent de Paul (1580–1660) — Founder. Patron of charitable groups.

St. Vincent Ferrer (1350–1419) — Dominican prior. Patron of builders, pavement workers, plumbers.

St. Vincent Pallotti (1795–1850) — Founder.

Notes

1. Doctor of the Church is a special title given by the Church to certain saints whose teachings and writings are seen as useful to Christians throughout the ages.
2. Referring to members, both male and female, of religious orders.
3. Referring to a man or woman who founded a religious order.